THE
CORONATION

A ROYAL HISTORY

Above: St Edward's Crown.

Above: Her Majesty Queen Elizabeth II processes down the nave of Westminster Abbey following her Coronation, on 2 June 1953.

Opposite: The Queen, moments after her crowning, holds the Rod of 'equity and mercy' and the Sceptre, signifying justice.

THE
CORONATION

A ROYAL HISTORY

ANNIE BULLEN

DUNDURN
TORONTO

Contents

Opposite: Her Majesty Queen Elizabeth II and Prince Philip, Duke of Edinburgh, photographed on 2 June 1953.

The Coronation Service

Her Majesty Queen Elizabeth II was crowned in historic Westminster Abbey, as have been kings and queens since the coronation of the Norman, William I, on Christmas Day in 1066. The first recorded Christian anointing and crowning, however, was in AD 786 when the Anglo-Saxon Offa, King of Mercia, had his son Egfrith appointed as his successor. That ceremony probably took place at what is now Chelsea, in London, and it is thought this was the first time that the anointing, a Frankish custom, had happened in Britain. The anointing has been a central part of the Coronation ceremony since that time.

Left: Depiction of the Coronation of a king from the *Litlyngton Missal*.

Two precious manuscripts, the *Liber Regalis* and the *Missal of Abbot Litlyngton,* are held in Westminster Abbey library. The former is an illuminated order of service, probably used by the monarchs themselves from Henry IV to Elizabeth I. This, one of the library's greatest treasures, was made around 1382, probably for the coronation of Richard II's queen, Anne of Bohemia. The *Litlyngton Missal,* commissioned in 1383 by Nicholas de Litlyngton, Abbot of Westminster between 1362 and 1386, gives details and depicts beautiful illuminated illustrations of great occasions at the Abbey, including the ceremonial procedure at coronations of British monarchs.

Left: Coronation of a queen, shown in the *Litlyngton Missal.*

Right: Coronation of a queen from the *Liber Regalis*.

A succession of coronations took place at Kingston-upon-Thames (in Surrey) in the 10th century. The clue is in the name of the town – 'King's Stone'. The original coronation stone, upon which seven Saxon kings are said to have been crowned, can still be seen outside the town's Guildhall.

The chronicles of history recount the coronations of Edgar (973) in Bath Abbey and Edward the Confessor at Winchester (in Hampshire) in 1043. Although Edward was crowned in Winchester, he is particularly associated with Westminster Abbey, the church that he devoted much of his life to rebuilding. He was canonized a century after his death in 1066 and his body moved to a shrine in the Abbey. His immediate successor, his brother-in-law Harold Godwineson – who became the first English king to die on the battlefield, losing his crown to William the

Conqueror – may or may not have been crowned at the Abbey for his short reign.

The Coronation service pre-dates the tradition of commemoration in Westminster Abbey. Several different types of consecration were used in England before Archbishop Dunstan, preparing to crown King Edgar in Bath Abbey in 973, devised the rite which is still largely used today. Small changes were made with the arrival of the Normans in 1066 but significant revisions were made in 1685 when the Catholic James II was crowned, and four years later with the joint enthronement of William and Mary. Then the Coronation Oath was altered to ensure that no Roman Catholic could be crowned in future and the taking of Holy Communion, phased out by James II, was reinstated. The crowning was made the final and main act of the Investiture.

Westminster Abbey

The magnificent Abbey church, built by Edward the Confessor and in which William I was crowned in 1066, was rebuilt almost two centuries later by the pious Plantagenet king Henry III, whose long reign of 56 years was remarkable for those times. He became passionate about architecture, especially admiring the great French cathedrals at Rheims, Chartres and Amiens and the Sainte-Chapelle in Paris. He was spurred on by veneration of his predecessor, Edward, whose saintliness he greatly revered, to rebuild Westminster Abbey in Gothic style. The Abbey had already become the Coronation church and Henry intended it to contain a shrine to the holy Confessor who had been canonized in 1161.

Edward's bones were moved to the magnificent shrine, built by Italian workmen, in October 1269. The stone base was embellished with wonderful decorative mosaic known as 'Cosmati work' after the Italian family of craftsmen who made it. The coffin containing the saint's remains was enclosed in a gold shrine, or 'feretory'. The whole was displayed under a wooden canopy and decorated with gold images of kings and saints. Around it were later built the tombs of eight medieval kings and queens, and for hundreds of years the shrine was a place of pilgrimage.

Today the shrine of Edward the Confessor lies in its Chapel, east of the Sanctuary at the heart of the Abbey. Although still impressive, it is much plainer than that built in the 13th century, assembled on a Purbeck marble base. The altar at the west end of the shrine, adorned with silver candlesticks given by The Queen's parents, King George VI

Left: Edward the Confessor, as depicted in one of the early 20th-century nave windows by Sir Ninian Comper.

Right: Westminster Abbey, the Coronation church.

Below: Westminster Abbey in 1547.

and Queen Elizabeth to mark their marriage, is used during the Coronation ceremony.

St Edward's Chapel, situated behind the High Altar, is where The Queen retired during her Coronation after she

One of the wonders of medieval England, the magnificent Cosmati 'pavement' in front of the High Altar, at the sacred heart of the Abbey, was long hidden under a covering but was restored in the early part of the 21st century. When Her Majesty Queen Elizabeth II was crowned here in 1953 the colourful pavement, glittering with pieces of purple porphyry, green serpentine, travertine and hundreds of thousands of tiny coloured glass tiles set in black Purbeck marble, was hidden beneath a thick carpet, intended to protect it. But modern conservators realized that it was doing the opposite, covering the precious mosaic with centuries of dirt and dust. Now the beautiful floor is on display on great state occasions, such as the wedding of the Duke and Duchess of Cambridge, in April 2011.

Right: A section of the Cosmati Pavement, in Westminster Abbey.

and the Duke of Edinburgh had taken Holy Communion towards the end of the ceremony. In the privacy of the Chapel she exchanged St Edward's Crown, which is used in the crowning ceremony, for the Imperial State Crown which symbolizes the authority of the monarchy. Assisted by her Maids of Honour, she donned her robe of embroidered purple velvet before beginning the long procession through the nave and out of the Abbey.

In all, 39 monarchs have been crowned in Westminster Abbey since 1066 – in 38 coronation ceremonies because in 1689 William and Mary, as joint rulers, were crowned together. There have also been 15 separate coronations of consorts – the last being that of Anne Boleyn in 1533.

Westminster Abbey was built primarily as the church for a monastery which housed 80 monks, and it was used by them rather than by a lay congregation. But it was to the Abbey that the nation turned for great ceremonial occasions, and since 1066 it has often been called the 'Coronation Church'. The reason lies in its architecture. Its great central space between the High Altar and the quire is the 'stage' where kings and queens are crowned. When Henry III asked master mason Henry of Reynes to design his new church it is probable that they based this central area on a similar design in Rheims Cathedral which they both admired and where French kings were once crowned. As at Rheims, Westminster Abbey's quire is placed west of the central crossing, truncating the nave but creating a vast space, almost a theatre in the round.

The Abbey's particular association with royalty was strengthened further in 1560 when Queen Elizabeth I

Above: Edward the Confessor's tomb, in Westminster Abbey.

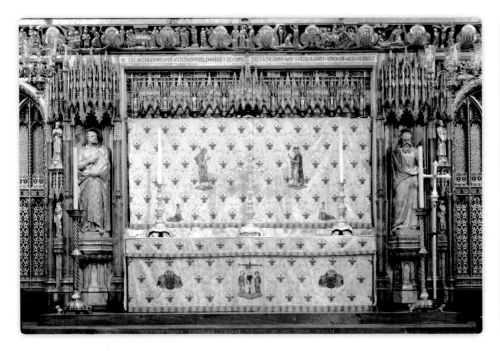

Above: The High Altar, prepared for the Coronation.

Above: King Edward's Chair, on which the Sovereign sits to be crowned.

Westminster Abbey's full name is The Collegiate Church of St Peter at Westminster and it is an abbey in name only. It was plundered of much of its treasure – including the gold cover of St Edward's coffin – sometime between 1536–40 when Henry VIII broke with the authority of the Church in Rome and assumed the title Supreme Head of the Church of England. In 1540 the monks had to sign the Deed of Surrender, handing their abbey over to the Crown, to become the cathedral of a new diocese. In fact, most of the monks were re-employed as the Dean and Chapter of the 'new' establishment. It is thought that Henry, who had already commissioned his tomb here, was anxious not to destroy his country's place of coronation.

Above: King George VI, at the moment of his crowning in Westminster Abbey, on 12 May 1937.

established it as a 'Royal Peculiar' – a church which falls under the direct and personal jurisdiction of the Sovereign.

The High Altar, designed by Sir George Gilbert Scott in 1867, is part of the Sanctuary, at the heart of the Abbey. The mosaic, depicting the Last Supper, behind the altar was made by Antonio Salviati. This forms part of the beautiful reredos, or screen, also designed by Gilbert Scott, in 1873 which includes four large statues of Moses, St Peter, St Paul and King David and the doors leading into St Edward's Chapel, which is immediately behind the screen.

The ancient Coronation Chair (King Edward's Chair), on which almost every British monarch since Edward II in 1308 has been crowned, stands in St George's Chapel – but without the ancient Stone of Destiny (or Stone of Scone), which was enclosed inside the chair when it was made on the orders of Edward I in 1300. The chair was painted with colourful birds, foliage and animals on a gilt background and an image of a king (either The Confessor or Edward I) on the back. In 1992, the Stone was returned to its ancient home in Edinburgh but it will be brought back to Westminster Abbey for future coronations.

The Coronation Ceremony

The structure of the Coronation ceremony was laid down in the 14th-century *Liber Regalis* (see pages 6–7). The procedures, which have been adapted over the centuries to suit the political and religious sensibilities of the time, are divided into six parts. These are: the Recognition, the Oath, the Anointing, the Investiture, the Homage, and the Holy Communion.

The Recognition • This is the only time that a Westminster Abbey congregation is required to shout – they are asked by the Archbishop of Canterbury to recognize, or acknowledge, the Sovereign, who is seated on the Chair of Estate, wearing the crimson velvet Robe of State and the crimson surcoat. The Archbishop says to those seated at the east, south, west and north of the Abbey:

'Sirs, I here present unto you King/Queen . . ., your undoubted King/Queen. Wherefore all you who are come this day to do your homage and service, are you willing to do the same?' Once the congregation has shouted its approval and the Sovereign has acknowledged their Recognition with a bow or curtsey, the Oath is taken.

The Oath • This is the Sovereign's pledge to serve the people and it is modified according to the circumstances of the times. The Sovereign is required, says the Coronation Oath Act of 1688, to 'Promise and Sweare to Governe the People of this Kingdome of England and the Dominions thereto belonging according to the Statutes in Parlyment Agreed on and the Laws and Customs of the same.'

In 1953 Queen Elizabeth II swore to govern the people of the United Kingdom, the Commonwealth and Northern Ireland 'according to their respective laws and customs', to 'cause law

Left: The clergy lead the Grand Procession into Westminster Abbey on Coronation Day in 1953. The Queen and her Maids of Honour follow them, along the nave.

There have been 15 separate coronations of consorts – but none for a long time. Henry VIII shared his coronation with that of his first wife, Catherine of Aragon, in 1509 but Anne Boleyn, his second wife, already pregnant with their daughter, the future Queen Elizabeth I, was crowned in a lavish ceremony at Westminster Abbey on 1 May 1533. She was the last queen consort to be crowned in a separate ceremony. Not all consorts are crowned – the first was Ælfthryth, wife of Edgar the Peaceful; they were anointed together in Bath in 973. William the Conqueror's wife, Matilda of Flanders, was the next consort to be crowned, in Westminster Abbey in 1068, two years after her husband.

and Justice, in Mercy,' to be executed in all her judgements and to preserve the integrity of the Church of England. Once the Oath has been sworn, a Bible is handed to the Sovereign with the words: 'Here is wisdom; this is the royal law; these are the lively oracles of God.' A King James Bible, including the Apocrypha, is used at this presentation. The Moderator of the Presbyterian Church of Scotland handed the Bible to The Queen in 1953. At this point the celebration of Holy Communion begins – but is interrupted as soon as the Nicene Creed has been said.

As soon as the anthem, readings and Creed are sung and said, the Communion service is interrupted, the Sovereign exchanging the plush ermine crimson and gold Robe of State for the Anointing Gown – a simple and austere plain white garment, full-skirted and fastening at the back and with no decoration. The scene is now set for the most sacred and secret part of the service, concealed from public gaze by the use of a canopy, held over the monarch by four Knights of the Garter.

The Anointing • Wearing the simple white robe, the Sovereign walks to St Edward's Chair – the Coronation Chair, with the Stone of Destiny placed in its base – and sits, as the golden canopy is raised overhead. The Dean pours the anointing oil from the Ampulla into the medieval Anointing Spoon and, steady-handed, holds it away from him for the Archbishop of Canterbury to dip into, using his thumb. The hands are anointed first and then, after another dip, the breast and head, while a prayer is said. The king or queen kneels for a blessing before the Investiture, in which the symbols of sovereignty are handed over.

The Investiture • First come the traditional robes of sovereignty – the Colobium Sindonis, a loose white under-robe of a fine linen-lawn cambric – the first robe with which the Sovereign is invested. It is edged with a

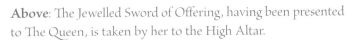

Above: The Jewelled Sword of Offering, having been presented to The Queen, is taken by her to the High Altar.

Left: Her Majesty, wearing a plain linen garment, sits in King Edward's Chair for the sacred moment of Anointing. The golden canopy hides her from public view during the ritual.

Right: Seated in the Coronation Chair, with St Edward's Crown on her head and holding the Rod and Sceptre, Her Majesty receives the Benediction.

beautifully worked lace border, open at the sides, sleeveless and cut low at the neck. It symbolizes the derivation of royal authority from the people. Over this goes the Supertunica – a long, gold silk, wide-sleeved coat flowing down to the ankles. It is lined with rose-coloured silk, trimmed with gold lace, woven with national symbols and fastened by a sword belt. Then the Spurs, representing chivalry, are presented followed by the Sword of State. More robes are assumed – the Robe Royal, an embroidered silver and crimson silk mantle and the Stole Royal, a richly embroidered and bejewelled gold scarf. The Archbishop delivers the Orb and a ring, representing the monarch's pledge to the nation. Two Sceptres – one surmounted by a Dove and one with a Cross – are presented, and these are

held in each hand by the Sovereign as the Archbishop of Canterbury carefully places St Edward's Crown on his or her head. This moment of crowning is the signal for the congregation to shout 'God Save the King/Queen' as they place their own coronets or caps on their heads.

The Homage • Now anointed and crowned, the monarch is led to the Throne, ready to receive homage, first from the Archbishop and the clergy, and then the Royal Family and the peers of the realm.

The Holy Communion • The service, begun before the Anointing, is resumed and completed before the Coronation ceremony ends.

The Coronation Regalia

At the heart of the collection of royal crowns, robes and ceremonial items known as the 'Crown Jewels' is the Coronation regalia, a group of valuable and symbolic pieces used, since the restoration of the monarchy in 1661, in the crowning ceremony of sovereigns of England. Today the Coronation regalia is kept, with the rest of the Crown Jewels, in the Jewel House in the Tower of London.

The original regalia, said to have been bequeathed by Edward the Confessor (1042–66) for all future coronations, was largely destroyed by Cromwell's men in 1649 during the Interregnum.

The Coronation regalia includes: the Ampulla, the Anointing Spoon, the Spurs, the Armills, the Jewelled Sword of Offering, the Orbs, the Rings and the Sceptres, each of which has considerable symbolic and historic significance in the ancient ceremony.

The Ampulla and the Coronation Spoon are used for the most solemn and sacred part of the ceremony where the Sovereign, hidden from public view, is anointed. The oil is kept in the gold Ampulla which takes the shape of a magnificent eagle. It stands about 8 inches (20cm) high. The master craftsman who fashioned the vessel in 1661 designed it so that the eagle's head can be unscrewed,

The silver-gilt Coronation Spoon was probably made in the late 12th century by a royal goldsmith. It was not destroyed during the Interregnum but sold for 16 shillings to Charles Kynnersley, one of Charles I's Wardrobe officials. Kynnersley returned the spoon in time for the coronation of Charles II in 1661, when it was embellished with the addition of four small pearls.

Left: The Ampulla, into which the Anointing oil is poured.

Right: The original Anointing or Coronation Spoon.

allowing the Ampulla to be filled with oil which is poured from the bird's beak into the Coronation Spoon.

The Anointing or Coronation Spoon is 400 years older than the rest of the Coronation regalia (see panel). Its bowl is engraved with acanthus leaves, while the tapering handle is attached to the bowl by a decoration in the shape of a tiny monster's head.

The Spurs, like much of the regalia, were made in 1661 in the same style, but with different decoration, as the medieval pair that had been melted down. They are gold, with tiny heel spikes projecting from a Tudor rose. They signify knighthood and the efforts of the knight to 'earn his spurs'.

The Jewelled Sword of Offering is one of four swords carried in the Abbey at the Coronation. The two Swords of Justice (Temporal and Spiritual) and the Sword of Mercy are carried, unsheathed and pointing skywards, during the procession, but play no part in the service. The Sword of Offering, used during the Investiture of the Sovereign, is a reminder that good should be protected and evil punished. The sword used today was made for the coronation of George IV in 1821 at a cost of almost £6,000 (£470,000 in today's value). Its hilt is covered with diamonds and emeralds, representing oak leaves, while the gold-covered leather scabbard is set with sapphires, rubies, emeralds and 1,200 diamonds in the shape of plants native to Great Britain.

The Armills represent sincerity and wisdom and are ancient symbols of nobility and military prowess. Their use in the Coronation ceremony was restored by Queen Elizabeth II in 1953 (see panel).

The Sovereign's Ring was made for William IV in 1831. It is unmistakable: a large sapphire, surrounded by 14 diamonds and with five rubies set over the sapphire in the shape of St George's Cross. Traditionally, the ring was regarded as the personal possession of the king or queen and a new one made for each coronation ceremony. A new ring was fashioned for Queen Victoria. However, George IV's magnificent ring and that of his wife, Queen Adelaide, were left to Victoria who, in turn, bequeathed

Below: The hollow gold Orb is set with precious stones, pearls and a large amethyst.

Right: The Sovereign's Sceptre with Dove (sometimes known as the Rod).

The Armills (or bracelets) of Queen Elizabeth II may have been the first used since before the restoration of the monarchy in 1661. A new pair was made for Charles II in that year, but it is thought that these golden bracelets with fine enamelling have never been worn. The 22-carat-gold Armills made for Queen Elizabeth in 1953, with their tiny Tudor rose clasps, were used in her crowning ceremony, and were a gift from the countries of the Commonwealth.

them and her own ring to the Crown. The large Sovereign's Ring has been used in every 20th-century coronation, including that of Queen Elizabeth II.

The Sovereign's Orb, originally a Roman emblem to signify imperial rule over the world, became a Christian symbol with the addition of a cross atop the sphere. It is given to the monarch during the Investiture as a reminder that the world serves Christ. The Sovereign's Orb, used at every coronation since 1661, is a magnificent and precious object, made of gold and set with pearls, emeralds, sapphires, rubies, one amethyst and 365 diamonds.

The Sceptres, sometimes known as 'Rods,' are offered to the Sovereign during the crowning ceremony and held, one in each hand, as St Edward's Crown is placed on his or her head. The Sovereign's Sceptre with Cross, made for Charles II in 1661, symbolizes the royal power of command, while the Sceptre with Dove, made at the same time, is a reminder of the duty of pastoral care. The former is placed in the monarch's right hand while the other is held in the left. A major and spectacular change to the Sceptre with Cross was made in 1910 when the largest top-quality cut diamond in the world was added to it. The 530-carat Cullinan I came from a huge chunk of diamond found in South Africa in 1905 and sent to England by parcel post, while a decoy diamond travelled on a heavily guarded ship. Once cut, the diamond yielded nine major stones which all eventually became part of the Crown Jewels or The Queen's personal jewellery collection. A decorative jewelled enamelled band, now at the bottom of the sceptre, was originally set higher up but was moved in 1838, to allow Queen Victoria to grasp the heavy sceptre firmly in the middle during her coronation.

Right: The Sovereign's Ring (left), decorated with a cross made of rubies, is placed on the monarch's fourth finger during the Coronation ceremony. The Queen Consort's ruby and diamond ring (right) was made for Queen Adelaide, wife of William IV, in 1831.

Above: The Armills, or bracelets, made for The Queen and given by the people of the Commonwealth for the Coronation ceremony.

Above: The original Armills, made for Charles II in 1661 but probably never used.

Above: St Edward's Crown, the Coronation crown.

Below: Queen Elizabeth II wearing St Edward's Crown, the Coronation crown.

Below: On 2 June 1953 Queen Elizabeth was crowned
'Elizabeth the Second, by the Grace of God, of Great Britain
and Northern Ireland and of her other Realms and Territories,
Queen, Head of the Commonwealth, Defender of the Faith.'
Coronation portrait by Cecil Beaton.

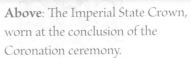

Above: The Imperial State Crown,
worn at the conclusion of the
Coronation ceremony.

In 1660 a committee, whose members included the newly returned King Charles II, convened to discuss regalia for his forthcoming coronation. The principal herald, Sir Edward Walker, advised that, as in medieval times, there should be two crowns used in the ceremony – a coronation crown and a state crown. One of these would be called 'St Edward's Crowne' and the other an 'Imperiall Crowne.'

Left: The Stole made for Queen Elizabeth II, for her Coronation in 1953.

Below: The Coronation Mantle.

The Coronation Crown, or St Edward's Crown, made in 1660–61 and still used today, was the most important piece of the regalia. Gold headbands, crosses, arches and fleur-de-lys were made and fitted together to form the outline while the jewels, inserted from behind and held in place by gold collars, were fitted through this frame. The stones were not meant to be permanent but were 'hired' from jewellers for the occasion and returned in the weeks after the ceremony. Queen Victoria did not use the crown for her coronation and it was only in 1902, when King Edward VII was determined to wear his namesake's crown, that it was retrieved and refurbished – only to be put aside again. Edward's coronation was postponed because of his appendicitis and, when he was

In 1296 King Edward I took the ancient Scottish Stone of Destiny (or Stone of Scone), on which Scottish kings were traditionally crowned, to Westminster Abbey. Four years later he ordered that a chair be made to enclose the rectangular block of sandstone. This wooden chair, known as King Edward's Chair or 'The Coronation Chair,' was decorated by Master Walter, a court painter. On Christmas Day in 1950 Scottish nationalists conspired to steal the Stone (breaking a piece off in the process). It was recovered four months later but the disagreement about its ownership remained. Eventually, in 1996, the British government decided that the Stone should be returned to Scotland. On 15 November of that year there was a ceremonial handover of the Stone of Destiny at the English/Scottish border. It was taken to Edinburgh Castle, where it is displayed in the Crown Room. An agreement has been reached to bring it back to Westminster for future coronations.

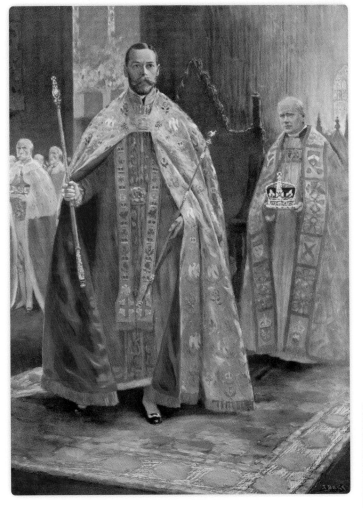

crown has been re-made three times since the Restoration; it is used on many state occasions and it contains many precious jewels, including Cullinan II, the second largest cut-diamond in the world.

The Coronation Robes: after the Anointing, the Sovereign puts on the cloth-of-gold Supertunica – a long silk ankle-length coat, belted at the waist and lined with deep pink silk. Over this is placed the Stole, a richly embroidered gold scarf, made in 1953 for Queen Elizabeth II. The Mantle, the magnificent cloak made for George IV in 1821, has been worn by The Queen, her father and grandfather.

well enough to undertake the ceremony, St Edward's Crown was deemed to be too heavy. But it came into its own for the coronation of George V in 1911 when it was reset with 444 semi-precious stones. It was also used for the crowning of Queen Elizabeth II's father, George VI, in 1937 and again for The Queen herself in 1953.

The Imperial State Crown is used for the concluding part of the Coronation service when it replaces St Edward's Crown, which is placed on the altar, and the Sovereign, wearing the purple robes of state and carrying the Orb and Sceptre, processes out of the Abbey. This magnificent

The Story of the Coronation

From earliest times a collection of ceremonial objects has been associated with leadership. The priceless 'treasure' found in the Sutton Hoo ship burial in 1939, believed to have belonged to King Raedwald who died in 625, contained an astonishing ceremonial helmet, gold and jewelled clasps and buckles, made with extraordinary skill, as well as a sceptre and finely wrought sword and shield, all clearly belonging to a man of power and authority.

There was no crown in this 'regalia', but there were two silver 'christening spoons' – Raedwald had been baptized, although he still kept a pagan altar alongside his Christian one. However, the rulers who followed him were converts and the concept of a Christian coronation, with the twin ideas of a crowning and an anointing with holy oils while being invested with royal regalia, became the tradition in 7th- and 8th-century Europe.

By the time Edward the Confessor, the last Anglo-Saxon king, died without an heir in 1066, the concept of a Christian ceremony to legitimize the authority of the new ruler, was well established. The Norman, William the Conqueror, emerged victorious in the scramble for the kingdom that followed Edward's death. He was crowned on a high stage at the crossing in Westminster Abbey on Christmas Day in 1066.

His successor, bellicose William Rufus – who died, shot by an arrow while hunting in the New Forest in 1100 – was crowned in Westminster Abbey, as was his brother, Henry I. Henry named his daughter, Matilda, as successor but Henry's nephew, Stephen, fought his way to the throne and was crowned in 1135. The civil war that followed ended in an agreement that Matilda's son, Henry II, should succeed the weak Stephen.

Below: Mourners carry the body of Edward the Confessor to the newly built Westminster Abbey, in this detail from the Bayeux Tapestry.

William I was consecrated on 25 December 1066 by Ealdred, Archbishop of York because the Archbishop of Canterbury, Stigand, refused to officiate at the coronation ceremony in Westminster Abbey. The new king sat on a six-foot (2-m) high platform, but when the congregation shouted their approval his guards, who had been stationed outside, thought a riot had started and they made matters worse by setting fire to the surrounding buildings, causing panic which emptied the Abbey.

Above: The Coronation of William I, from *Anciennes Chroniques d'Angleterre* by Jean Batard de Wavrin.

Left: The royal seal of Richard the Lionheart.

Above: Kings of England – Henry II, Richard I, King John and Henry III, from *The Kings of England from Brutus to Henry III*.

By this time, the idea of a king's regalia was accepted, but the items were not passed from ruler to ruler – until the monks of Westminster Abbey made the claim that Edward the Confessor had asked that his regalia, which was in their safekeeping, should be used in all future coronations. Scholars say that The Confessor, canonized in 1161, probably made no such bequest, and the monks, hoping to attract pilgrims, fabricated the story. By 1216, however, when the Plantagenet king, 13-year-old Henry III, succeeded to the throne, the crown used in his coronation was said to have belonged to Edward the Confessor. Again, there is no proof that this was so, but it became known as St Edward's Crown from that date and was used until the destruction of the regalia at the time of the Civil War. The coronation of Henry III in 1216 – who rebuilt Westminster Abbey with a shrine for Edward the Confessor, and was himself buried there in 1272 – saw the beginning of a hereditary collection of regalia.

The Plantagenets

With the death of Stephen in 1154 came the first Plantagenet king, Henry II. This French-born Angevin monarch, son of Matilda and thus grandson of the Norman, Henry I, became the most powerful sovereign in medieval Europe, with a kingdom stretching from Ireland to the Pyrenees. His line, the Plantagenets, which embraced the Angevins and the houses of York and Lancaster, is the longest in English history, lasting 330 years to Richard III.

Although Henry reputedly hated ceremonial occasions, his coronation, in 1154, in Westminster Abbey, was doubly splendid as he was the first English king to be crowned with his queen consort, his wife, Eleanor of Aquitaine. His nickname of 'Curtmantle' probably dated from this time, as he appeared for the ceremony wearing a doublet and a short Angevin cloak or mantle.

Henry's sons had spent much of his reign plotting against him and each other. He was succeeded by Richard, known as the Lionheart, who spoke no English and who spent only six months of his ten-year reign in England. His coronation, in 1189, was a prelude to a long stay away on crusade. He returned in 1194 after many adventures, including being captured and released on the payment of a huge ransom. Staying just long enough to be re-crowned and to settle a dispute with his brother John, Richard was not seen in England again. He died of a crossbow wound in 1199, to be succeeded by the unpopular John. Reports of John's coronation in May 1199 show that he displayed 'unseemly levity' during the ceremony, when he left before taking Holy Communion.

John's eldest son Henry III proved a better king than his father, or uncle. He was only nine when he was hastily crowned at Gloucester Abbey in 1216, but he underwent a more formal ceremony at Westminster in 1220. (Gloucester Abbey ceased to have monks in 1541 when Henry VIII ordered the dissolution of monasteries, but the

Above: The crowning of the boy-king Richard II in 1377. This life-size painting, in Westminster Abbey, is the earliest portrait of a reigning monarch.

buildings became a cathedral with a Dean and Chapter in 1541.) It was Henry III, champion of architecture, who rebuilt Westminster Abbey (see pages 8–11). He and his son Edward I ('Longshanks') reigned for 91 years between them, creating a stable monarchy. Edward, an enthusiastic soldier, was on crusade when his father died in 1272 and it was not until 1274 that he was crowned.

The first coronation procession was that of Richard II (reigned 1377–99) who rode from the Tower of London to Westminster, setting a precedent that was followed thereafter. The last in the long line of Plantagenets was Richard III, whose reputation as a black-hearted dastard is periodically questioned. On his coronation day in 1483 he and his wife, Anne Neville, showed humility when they walked barefoot on a red carpet to the Abbey.

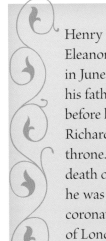

Henry 'The Younger', son of Henry II and Eleanor of Aquitaine was given a coronation in June 1170, to settle the succession during his father's lifetime. However Henry died before his father, leaving his two brothers, Richard and then John, to succeed to the throne. Edward V, who succeeded on the death of his father Edward IV in1483 when he was just 12 years of age, did not have a coronation – he was thrown into the Tower of London with his brother Richard – and never seen again. His uncle, Richard III, was the prime suspect in the boys' disappearance.

Here doth Erl Rivers with hys good prynters William Caxton present hys book unto ye King hys Maiestys

Above: King Edward IV (1442–83) who is shown here being given the first book printed in England. The book is *Dictes or Sayeings of the Philosophres* (1477) and it is presented by the printer William Caxton.

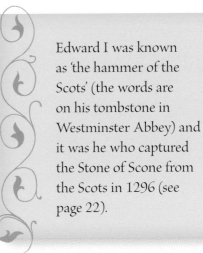

Edward I was known as 'the hammer of the Scots' (the words are on his tombstone in Westminster Abbey) and it was he who captured the Stone of Scone from the Scots in 1296 (see page 22).

Left: The Coronation of Henry IV (1399–1413) from Froissart's *Chronicle*.

The Tudors

Richard III, the last Plantagenet, was hastily crowned on the day set aside for the coronation of his nephew, the young Edward V, who, along with his brother, was declared illegitimate, imprisoned in the Tower of London and never seen again. Richard's only son, Edward of Middleham, Prince of Wales, had died, aged 10, in 1484. Richard nominated his nephew, John, Earl of Lincoln, as his heir but a certain Henry Tudor, Earl of Richmond, whose own claim to the throne was weak, challenged him in battle in the ongoing 'Wars of the Roses'. Henry's mother, Lady Margaret Beaufort, was descended from John of Gaunt, but in a line barred from the succession, while his father, Edmund Tudor, was the son of Henry V's widow, Catherine de Valois and Owen Tudor. Henry, who supported the Lancastrian side in the Wars of the Roses, invaded England in August 1485 and defeated and killed Richard at Bosworth field in the same month. It is said that Henry VII underwent an impromptu crowning in the village of Stoke Golding near the battlefield, using a battered coronet that had belonged to the slain Richard.

The official coronation, heralding the first of the Tudor kings and queens, took place just two months later, at Westminster Abbey. Henry married Elizabeth of York early the following year, thus uniting the warring factions of Lancaster and York. Henry's reign saw the establishment of a prudent government, forming trade links with Europe and bringing peace and security to England. Henry's death in 1509 saw his younger son, the 18-year-old Henry VIII accede to the throne. Arthur, the first son, had died in 1502 and the young Henry married his widow, Catherine of Aragon.

'Our time is spent in continuous festival,' wrote Catherine to her father, after she and her new husband, Henry VIII, were married on 11 June 1509 at the Franciscan church at Greenwich, and then crowned on Midsummer's Day, 24 June at Westminster Abbey. But that was not to last, as Henry re-married – five times. Henry was succeeded, in 1547, by his only legitimate son, Edward VI, whose mother Jane Seymour, Henry VIII's third wife, had died in 1537, just after his birth. Edward, only nine, was crowned in a shortened ceremony because of his youth, four days after his father's funeral. Unfortunately he died just six years later and, although he had nominated Lady Jane Grey as his successor, she was deposed (and executed) after nine days on the throne, with no time for a coronation. Mary Tudor, Henry's elder daughter, became queen, being crowned in 1553, the first English queen to have a coronation in her own right.

Left: Henry Tudor (King Henry VII) and his wife, Elizabeth of York, are buried together in a magnificent Lady Chapel in Westminster Abbey. Their gilt bronze effigies lie on the tomb.

Right: This painting, by
Lucas de Heere, of Henry VIII
shows the Tudor succession –
Henry himself, his son
Edward VI and his daughters,
Mary and Elizabeth.

Left: A portrait of Queen Elizabeth I in her coronation robes, from a painting by an unknown artist.

It is not known when Henry VIII altered his Coronation Oath, but the wording was changed, in his own hand, on the original manuscript, presumably to conform with what he saw as his Royal Supremacy over the Church, following his break with Rome in the 1530s. There are several significant revisions, including a change to the Oath to maintain the rights and liberties of the 'holy churche' with Henry's qualification 'nott preiudyciall to his jurysdyction and dignite ryall ...'.

Like her step-brother, Edward, she wore three crowns during the ceremony – St Edward's Crown, the Imperial Crown and a smaller crown, made especially for her.

She was succeeded in 1558 by her half-sister, Elizabeth, the last of the Tudor monarchs, whose long reign is remembered for victory over the Spanish Armada and the great flowering of English culture and exploration. Elizabeth was crowned on 15 January 1559. The service, although the last to be performed as a Catholic mass, did have significant changes such as the reading of the Epistle and Gospel in English rather than Latin, while the consecrated host was not elevated for veneration. Mary Tudor had the Archbishop of Canterbury, Thomas Cranmer, executed in 1556 and no new Archbishop had been appointed. All the senior bishops appointed by Mary refused to officiate, so Elizabeth was crowned by the Bishop of Carlisle, Owen Oglethorpe.

Above: The coronation procession of King Edward VI from the
Tower of London to Cheapside, in 1547.

The Stuarts and House of Orange

Elizabeth I, who was much mourned, had died childless in 1603. Her refusal to marry ensured her independence, but made her the last of the Tudors. The Stuart dynasty that followed saw the union of the two crowns of Scotland and England, the (temporary) abolishing of the monarchy, the only husband and wife to rule jointly, and the eventual union, in 1707, of Scotland and England to form Great Britain.

Elizabeth's successor, James VI of Scotland, was the son of Elizabeth's cousin, the Catholic Mary, Queen of Scots, whose execution Elizabeth had reluctantly ordered in 1587. James, a Protestant, had succeeded to the Scottish throne when a very young child in 1567, on his mother's abdication. He was crowned James I of England at Westminster Abbey in 1603, seated on the Coronation Chair with the Stone of Destiny, the ancient coronation stone of the Scots, placed underneath.

He survived the Roman Catholic Gunpowder Plot in 1605 and was succeeded by his son Charles I, in 1625, when things began to go horribly wrong for the monarchy. Charles, who believed in the divine right of kings to rule as they wished, failed to call a parliament for 11 years. When Parliament did eventually meet, grievances were aired and two factions, the Parliamentarians, under leaders such as Oliver Cromwell, and the Royalists, began raising armies

Below: James I, King of England and Scotland (portrayed as James VI), from a portrait by Paul van Somer.

Samuel Pepys wrote this account of the coronation of Charles II:

'At last comes in the Deane and prebends of Westminster with the Bishops (many of them in cloth-of-gold Copes); and after them the nobility all in their parliament-robes, which was a most magnificent sight. Then the Duke and the King with a scepter (carried by my Lord of Sandwich) and Sword and mond before him, and the crowne too.

The King in his robes, bare headed, which was very fine. And after all had placed themselfs – there was a sermon and the service. And then in the Quire at the high altar he passed all the ceremonies of the Coronacion'.

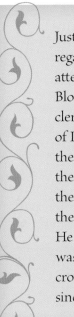

Just ten years after the new Coronation regalia was made for Charles II, there was an attempt to steal it by Irish colonel Thomas Blood. In 1671, the adventurer, dressed as a clergyman, tricked his way into the Tower of London room where St Edward's Crown, the Orb and Sceptre were kept. He knocked the guard unconscious and made off with the precious crown squashed into a bag and the Orb reputedly stuffed down his breeches. He was swiftly arrested but, following a trial, was pardoned by King Charles. The damaged crown was repaired and has been used ever since in the Coronation ceremony.

WILHELMUS REX. & MARIA REGINA.

and thus began the civil war of 1642. Charles was defeated, tried for treason and beheaded on 30 January 1649.

Oliver Cromwell, who introduced a Puritan regime, sat on the Coronation Chair for his inauguration as Lord Protector. On his death – and after the Coronation regalia had been sold, melted down and destroyed by the Puritans – Charles II, son of the executed king, was recalled from exile. Glorious new regalia was made for his coronation on 23 April 1661.

Charles was succeeded in 1685 by his brother James II, whose coronation was marred by bad omens – the crown slipped from his head and, at the moment of crowning, the Royal Standard at the Tower of London was ripped apart by the wind. There was no Holy Communion, as James,

a Catholic, had been anointed and crowned following Catholic rite in the chapel at Whitehall the day before. His Catholic policies impelled politicians to 'invite' William of Orange and his wife (James's Protestant daughter) Mary, to claim the throne. They overthrew James and became joint rulers in 1689. A new coronation chair and crown were made for Mary. During the Investiture, their coronation rings were mixed up and Mary's ruby was placed on William's finger. They were a devoted couple. Mary died in 1694 and William ruled alone, until a fall from his horse killed him in 1702. He was succeeded by Mary's sister, Anne, who was crowned in April 1702, having been carried into the Abbey on an open chair by the Yeomen of the Guard because of her gout.

House of Hanover

For the second time in 30 years a foreign monarch was crowned king in Westminster Abbey. George of Hanover (Queen Anne's second cousin) spoke not a word of English on his accession to the throne in 1714 and learnt very little more during the whole of his reign. His coronation, on 20 October that year, was conducted mostly in Latin because of the language problems. He was a deeply unpopular king.

His son, George II (with whom he was not on good terms) was much more popular with the British people. Although he was the last British monarch to be born outside the United Kingdom, he did speak English. He also had a difficult relationship with his eldest son, Frederick (who died after an accident in 1751) and was succeeded by his grandson, George III. At last here was a king born in Britain and professing himself to

The magnificent gathering, waiting to begin the coronation banquet for George IV in Westminster Hall, fell silent as an imposing figure, in full armour, rode into the hall on horseback, throwing down a gauntlet to challenge anyone to deny the new Sovereign. This was Sir Henry Dymock, whose family had held the hereditary post of King's Champion since 1377. The 1821 coronation was the last time this ceremony has been performed in full. Colonel Sir John Marmion Dymock, Queen's Champion, was present at the Coronation of Queen Elizabeth in 1953.

love the country. His long reign (60 years) was disrupted by periods of mental illness and his son, yet another George, became Prince Regent in 1811, succeeding his father to the throne in 1820 in what was arguably the most extravagant coronation in the history of the British monarchy.

George IV, unlike his father, did not have a happy marriage (his wife, Caroline, was barred from his coronation) and had led the life of a roué, squandering his talents on drinking, gambling and womanizing. He was responsible for the architectural extravaganza that is Brighton Pavilion. He died, enormously fat, after just ten years on the throne and the succession passed to his brother, the 64-year-old William, Duke of Clarence, a bluff and genial sailor. William IV and Queen Adelaide were crowned, he wearing his admiral's uniform, in September 1831. The new king, who declared his reluctance to have a costly ceremony, decided that this time there should be no banquet, because of the expense. William was the last British king of Hanover as his cousin and heir, Victoria, a woman, could not become ruler there.

Right: King George IV, from a portrait by Sir Thomas Lawrence.

George IV, forever known as 'Prinny' from his long years as the extravagant Prince Regent, spent £240,000 (£19 million in today's value) on his coronation in 1821. His tailor was sent to Paris to make a copy of Napoleon's coronation robe, so thickly embroidered and covered in fur that it took eight pages to lift it behind him – with the fear that, had they dropped it, he would have toppled over. His new crown had 12,000 diamonds and the whole occasion made him sweat so much he used 19 handkerchiefs to mop away the perspiration.

Left: King George III wearing his coronation robes, a portrait by Allan Ramsay.

Hanover and Saxe-Coburg-Gotha

Princess Victoria was 18 years old when, in June 1837, she was woken at six in the morning in her room at Kensington Palace, and summoned, in her dressing gown, to be told by the Lord Chamberlain and Archbishop of Canterbury that she was Queen of England. She had suffered a dismal childhood, over-protected by a mother terrified she might mix with unsuitable people and determined to control her. When the young Victoria moved to Buckingham Palace she consigned her mother to a remote apartment.

Victoria was the last in the Hanoverian line of rulers, her father being Prince Edward, the Duke of Kent, the fourth son of George III. Edward died when Victoria, born in 1819, was only a few months old. William IV, Victoria's cousin, was determined to live long enough for the young woman to rule in her own right – he detested her overbearing and ambitious mother, Marie Louise Victoria, Duchess of Kent, who would have been regent had he died any time before Victoria's 18th birthday. As it was, he managed to survive just four weeks after she achieved this age on 24 May 1837. From the start Victoria undertook her new royal duties with composure and confidence – and without her mother overseeing every move. Before his death her cousin was overseeing the renovation of Buckingham House into a grand palace, but he died before this work was completed, leaving Victoria to be the first British monarch to live there.

She was crowned more than a year after she had succeeded to the throne, on 28 June 1838. The ceremony lasted for five hours and had not been rehearsed properly. It seems that no one apart from Victoria herself and Lord John Thinned, the acting Dean of Westminster, knew the order of service or what should be happening. Lord Rolle, an elderly peer, fell down the steps while making his homage to the young queen, who noted in her diary:

The name Saxe-Coburg-Gotha was brought to the British Royal Family when Victoria married her cousin, Prince Albert, whose father, Ernst was Duke of Saxe-Coburg and Gotha. Queen Victoria remained a Hanoverian, but their son, Edward, who was Victoria's successor, took his father's line, becoming the only British monarch of the House of Saxe-Coburg-Gotha.

Above: King William IV, Princess Victoria's cousin, painted by Sir William John Newton.

'Poor old Lord Rolle, who is 82 and dreadfully infirm, in attempting to ascend the steps fell and rolled quite down, but was not the least hurt; when he attempted to re-ascend them I got up and advanced to the end of the steps in order to prevent another fall.'

The excited 19-year-old, who rushed back to her rooms at Buckingham Palace to bathe her beloved spaniel, Dash, as soon as the service was over, also noted that the Archbishop of Canterbury had not put the coronation ring on the correct finger:

'The Archbishop had (most awkwardly) put the ring on the wrong finger, and the consequence was that I had the greatest difficulty to take it off again, which I at last did with great pain ....'

Nevertheless she clearly enjoyed the ceremony, recording the day in detail and calling it: 'The proudest of my life.'

House of Saxe-Coburg-Gotha

Although Victoria had led an isolated and confined childhood, she and her beloved Albert restricted their eldest son, Albert Edward ('Bertie') in the same way, forcing him to study (and inculcating an intense dislike of books), and limiting his personal freedom. When he did finally 'escape' to study at Cambridge, he relished his freedom and made the most of it.

His father, hearing of his excesses, went to visit Bertie, using his position as Chancellor of the University as an excuse. But Bertie, who was keeping a young woman in his Cambridge rooms, paid no heed and Prince Albert, tired, cold and travelling in the pouring rain, contracted what was at first thought to be a chill and then diagnosed as typhoid. He died in December 1861, soon after his fruitless visit to Cambridge. It was several years before Prime Minister Benjamin Disraeli could coax Victoria back to public duty. Bertie, Prince of Wales for longer than any of his predecessors, was allowed to make official overseas visits, including to Canada and North America and the Middle East and, later, India, but given no other

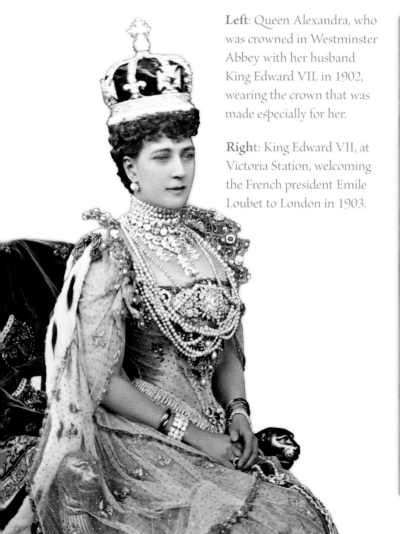

Left: Queen Alexandra, who was crowned in Westminster Abbey with her husband King Edward VII, in 1902, wearing the crown that was made especially for her.

Right: King Edward VII, at Victoria Station, welcoming the French president Emile Loubet to London in 1903.

responsibilities. He was married to the beautiful Danish princess, Alexandra, but had several mistresses and enjoyed a life of music halls and parties.

When Victoria died, in 1901, there were no great hopes for Edward VII's reign, but he became a surprisingly good ambassador for Britain, a natural diplomat. He cut a dash in uniform, sat well on a horse and was able to contribute to foreign policy, fostering good relations with other countries, notably France, with whom he engineered the signing of the *entente cordiale* and for which he became known as 'peacemaker'. Edward turned out to be one of the most popular kings the country has known. His reign coincided with the start of a new century and saw significant changes. Powered flight was made possible at this time, while Edward encouraged the modernization of the British Home Fleet and the reorganization of the British Army. Royalty and guests from all over Europe were invited to the coronation of Edward and Alexandra, scheduled for June 1902.

Edward VII's coronation in 1902 was postponed at the last minute, as he was taken ill with appendicitis. When the ceremony finally took place, two months later, it was suggested, to avoid tiring him, that only his hands should be anointed, rather than the hands, head and breast. But he demurred: 'If I am going to be done, I am going to be done properly.'

As the Sovereign processes from the west end of Westminster Abbey, through the nave and quire to the High Altar, in the first part of the Coronation service, verses from Psalm 122, with the words: 'I was glad when they said unto me: We will go into the house of the Lord', have traditionally been sung and several musical settings of these words have been used over the centuries. It was at the coronation of Edward VII that Sir Hubert Parry's version received its first performance and it has been used ever since. Parry incorporated into it the cries of 'Vivat Rex!' and 'Vivat Regina!' with which the scholars of Westminster School traditionally acclaim the Sovereign.

Right: King Edward VII, from a portrait by Sir Samuel Luke Fildes.

Coronation luncheon for King George V and Queen Mary, in the Guildhall, London, 29 June 1911, a painting by Solomon J. Solomon.

House of Windsor

George, the second son of Edward VII and Queen Alexandra, had followed a naval career because it was assumed that his elder brother, Albert Edward, the Duke of Clarence, would become king. Unfortunately 'Eddy,' as he was known, died in the influenza epidemic of 1892, leaving George to become king in 1910, assuming the crown and also marrying his brother's fiancée, Mary of Teck.

The sailor-king George V committed himself fully to a British way of life. In 1917, as a result of the anti-German feeling of the First World War, he changed the family name from the House of Saxe-Coburg-Gotha to 'Windsor.' He also decreed that the titles 'Prince' and 'Princess' should be given only to the children and grandchildren of the Sovereign, and that the titles 'Highness' and 'Serene Highness' should be allowed to die out. His coronation, on 22 June 1911, was the first where photographs were taken within Westminster Abbey.

Having reigned throughout the First World War, King George died three years before the Second World War, leaving the throne to his eldest son, the playboy Prince Edward. He became King Edward VIII for just 11 months, before abdicating to marry the American divorcee Mrs Simpson, and throwing the monarchy into disarray. 'After I am dead the boy will ruin himself in 12 months,' King George is reported to have said of his eldest son, with some justification. Edward did not receive a coronation.

Edward's younger brother, another sailor-king who saw action at the Battle of Jutland, was christened Albert, but became King George VI. Poor George was dismayed. He was shy, had a stammer and lacked confidence. He was

The term 'family firm' was coined by George VI and is still used by the Royal Family themselves when they are describing the division of the public duties carried out by the family members.

Left: King George V in 1911 at the 'Delhi Durbar,' in India, a mass assembly to commemorate his coronation.

married to the Scottish commoner, Elizabeth Bowes-Lyon. They already had two young children when they were crowned in Westminster Abbey on 12 May 1937, the day that had been planned for his brother's coronation. In the Royal Gallery at the Abbey were his mother, Queen Mary, and his two daughters, Princess Elizabeth (who by this twist of fate was now heir presumptive to the throne) and the younger Princess Margaret.

Despite his own and the country's misgivings about his fitness to rule, George VI did so with a sense of duty that impressed and won the hearts of a nation at war. He and Queen Elizabeth gained respect for remaining in London during the Blitz, shared rationing and became figureheads for the beleaguered country, especially when Buckingham Palace took a direct hit from German bombs while they were in residence. 'Now I can look the East End in the face,' said the Queen. George died of lung cancer at the age of 56, in February 1952. His daughter, Princess Elizabeth, the Duchess of Edinburgh, who at the time was representing him on an overseas visit, was to become queen.

Right: The young Princess Elizabeth arrives at Westminster Abbey for the coronation of her father, King George VI, on 12 May 1937.

Below: The Royal Family on the balcony at Buckingham Palace, after the coronation of King George VI. Princess Elizabeth and Princess Margaret stand between their parents, Queen Elizabeth and King George.

Princess Elizabeth

At the age of 15, Princess Elizabeth Alexandra Mary became Colonel-in-Chief of the Grenadier Guards. She celebrated her 16th birthday by carrying out her first official engagement, an inspection of the regiment, thus beginning a round of duty and ceremony that would last for the rest of her life.

When she was born, on 21 April 1926, Elizabeth, the King's first grandchild, was reasonably expected to live the comfortable life of a junior member of the Royal Family – and so she did until she was 10 years old. She would have liked, she once said, to have been a lady living in the country with lots of horses and dogs. However, when her uncle, King Edward VIII, abdicated and her father was crowned King George VI, her training as next in line to the throne began in earnest.

By the time she was 18, Princess Elizabeth was given a private sitting room at Windsor Castle in which to receive visitors and had appointed her first lady-in-waiting and private secretary, Lady Mary Strachey. She became a Counsellor of State, one of the official representatives for her father when he was away. Unlike her father and grandfather, who had not expected to succeed to the throne, Elizabeth's teenage years and young adulthood was spent in learning every aspect of the British Constitution and in training for the life of duty that would be hers when she became queen.

Elizabeth was as steadfast in her affections as in her duty to her country. On the eve of the Second World War, as a slight 13-year-old girl, she met her distant cousin, the handsome young Prince Philip of Greece, who was 18 and a cadet at Dartmouth naval college. Elizabeth and her family, aboard the Royal Yacht *Victoria and Albert*, called in at Dartmouth where the tall fair-haired cadet, who was to capture her heart, was detailed to look after Elizabeth and her sister, Princess Margaret. The two cousins were regularly in touch after that meeting.

When the war was over Philip, who had spent some of his naval leave at Buckingham Palace during the hostilities,

Right: *Princess Elizabeth chats with a Guide Leader in Basutoland, on the royal tour of South Africa with her family in 1947.*

and Elizabeth began to see each other in earnest. By now, because of her father's failing health, the Princess had taken on many of his engagements – launching ships, appearing at public functions and taking the salute at military occasions. She and Philip, despite initial opposition from her parents, became secretly engaged on a summer holiday at Balmoral in late 1946. The King eventually agreed to their betrothal on condition that it was kept secret for a while longer.

Elizabeth spent her 21st birthday in South Africa where the Royal Family were on tour. She made a birthday broadcast from Government House, Cape Town, pledging herself to the service of the British Commonwealth: 'I declare before you all that my whole life, whether it be long or short, shall be devoted to your service,' she said. On her return, the engagement to Prince Philip was officially announced and the royal wedding date set for 20 November that year.

Above: The Princess makes a broadcast on 21 April 1947, her 21st birthday, from the gardens of Government House, Cape Town when she pledged her life to the service of the people of the British Commonwealth and Empire.

Right: Princess Elizabeth and Prince Philip, her fiancé, photographed at Buckingham Palace in January 1947.

The Duke and Duchess of Edinburgh

The wedding of Princess Elizabeth to Prince Philip, on 20 November 1947 at Westminster Abbey, was described by Winston Churchill, despite the cold, damp November weather, as 'a flash of colour on the hard road we travel' and it seems that the people of Britain thought so, too. Many people bought their first television sets to watch the royal wedding, while cards, presents and greetings from well-wishers poured in to Buckingham Palace for the young couple.

Just a year later their first child, Prince Charles, was born and the Duke and Duchess of Edinburgh settled in the newly renovated Clarence House, and to life as one of the country's most glamorous young couples. Princess Elizabeth knew that, once crowned queen, her life would belong to the nation. So when the chance came to live, if just for a few months, a 'normal' married life with her husband, she did not hesitate.

Prince Philip returned to active naval service in Malta a year after Prince Charles' birth and Princess Elizabeth flew out to join him. Although it must have been a wrench to leave her baby, she knew that the young Prince was well looked after by nursery staff and doting grandparents.

Above: Princess Elizabeth and the Duke of Edinburgh, shortly after their wedding, on 20 November 1947.

Above: Princess Elizabeth with her husband, Prince Philip in Malta, where he was stationed with the Royal Navy.

Elizabeth found life on Malta extraordinarily liberating. For the first time, she was able to lead a comparatively ordinary life, driving her own car, a Daimler, visiting the hairdresser, going on shopping expeditions, and joining in happily with the other Navy wives with their coffee mornings and drinks parties.

When Philip was on shore they would dine out and dance together at hotels and restaurants, and enjoy boating trips to local beaches and creeks, swimming, sunbathing and picnicking – just like everyone else.

When Princess Elizabeth returned to England early in 1950, she was expecting their second child, Princess Anne, who was born on 15 August. However, by May 1951 her father, the King, was clearly unwell. He underwent an operation for lung cancer which seemed to be successful, so his daughter and son-in-law represented him on a trip to Canada, with a short visit to the USA as guests of President Truman. The young couple came home to another round of engagements and ceremonial occasions, only relaxing at Christmas at King George's beloved Sandringham. All too soon, at the end of January 1952, they were off again, embarking, in the King's name, on a long tour to East Africa, Australia and New Zealand.

The sad news arrived in the early afternoon of 6 February. Philip and Elizabeth, on safari in Kenya, had spent the previous night at the spectacular Treetops, a cabin built high in a giant fig tree overlooking a watering-hole, where the animals of the East African plains came to drink by moonlight. The Duke and Duchess of Edinburgh watched rhino, elephant and waterbuck before driving back to Sagana Lodge on the lower slopes of Mount Kenya.

That afternoon Philip had to tell his wife that her father had died during the night. She had little time to show the grief she felt at the loss of a beloved father. Within an hour, the new queen was in a car speeding to the airport, to fly home and take up the duties that would be hers for the rest of her life.

Preparing for Coronation Day

In the grey February of Queen Elizabeth II's accession, post-war austerity still hung as a shadow over the country. So the Coronation was planned for June 1953, in the following year when it was hoped the weather would be bright and warm and there would be enough time to prepare Westminster Abbey for the ceremony.

Archbishop Geoffrey Fisher worked on the detailed liturgy for the service, using that of earlier coronations as a guide. He also devoted much time for preparing The Queen for the day, making her a 'Little Book' of private devotions, containing a month's worth of daily prayers and meditations to be read in the four weeks before the ceremony.

Members of the Armed Forces had some more unusual duties in connection with the Coronation. When the extra seating was finally in place in Westminster Abbey, they were asked to spend two hours sitting up and down on the seats and marking time on all the stands, to test their strength.

Above: Ceremonial uniforms for the Life Guards and Household Cavalry are fitted at Knightsbridge Barracks, in London, in preparation for the Coronation.

Above: Coronation flags and banners being sewn at Fladbury Mill, in Worcestershire.

Meanwhile, historic Westminster Abbey – the ancient Coronation church – was being transformed for the occasion. The seating would have to be increased to 8,000 and an Annexe built to accommodate the processions. The nave closed six months before Coronation Day (Christmas services went ahead in the quire and transepts) and, a month later, the whole of the Abbey was closed to allow the precious fabric to be protected before the building work began.

Seats, raked to the full height of the nave arcading, were tiered either side of the quire and nave, using hundreds of tonnes of wood and scaffolding. Three tiers in the transepts were assembled to seat Members of Parliament and the aristocracy. In the Coronation 'theatre', the place of crowning, the floor was raised, and a dais erected to accommodate the Throne. A total of 2,000 wooden chairs, upholstered in blue velour finished with gold braid and with the royal cipher embroidered on the backs, were made and brought in, while almost 6,000 stools were added to the nave seats. Press and broadcast facilities had to be arranged, too. The Queen's father,

The Annexe that was built at the west end of Westminster Abbey, planned by Minister of Works David Eccles, was not only a place for processions to assemble. There was also space for the Coronation regalia to be laid out, retiring rooms for the peers taking part in the procession, and separate robing rooms for The Queen and the Duke of Edinburgh. There was also a dining room, where The Queen and her family lunched after the service, before the long procession through London to Buckingham Palace.

King George VI, had allowed the radio microphones into his coronation in 1936, but this was the first to be televised. Drinking-water fountains were installed and ten medical centres discreetly set up, in case of sudden illness in the congregation. The blue and gold carpet for the nave, almost 120 feet (36m) long, 17 feet (5m) wide and weighing 5 tonnes, was made in Glasgow.

Left: Artists were kept busy painting beautifully detailed wall decorations for the Coronation.

Above: Artists designing flags for the Coronation, at Edgington's factory in Sidcup, Kent.

Past coronations had not always been the best-organized events, but this one was different – the television cameras were to be allowed in. The BBC had fought hard for the privilege, which was initially opposed by the Archbishop of Canterbury and The Queen herself. Special arrangements included fixing (gilded) sound microphones to the Throne, to the kneeling stool in front of the Chair of Estate, and to the Coronation Chair. One of the cameramen was positioned so near to the conductor of the orchestra that he felt his head being struck several times by the baton during the ceremony.

None of this was seen by the public, of course, because a series of comprehensive rehearsals meant there were few mishaps on the day. The Queen, wearing a crown so that she could become used to its weight, and robed in a sheet in place of the long velvet train, rehearsed at Buckingham Palace with her Maids of Honour, using a floor plan specially laid out for her.

The Queen's dress was designed by Norman Hartnell, who made the Coronation outfits for all the Royal Family and for her Maids of Honour. The Queen's white silk gown was embroidered with flowers representing each country of the British Isles and Commonwealth, including the English rose and the Scottish thistle, lotus flowers for India and Ceylon, and the maple leaf of Canada. Known only to Norman Hartnell and The Queen was a small four-leaf clover, embroidered on the left-hand side of the skirt, where it would be brushed by her hand during the ceremony.

Each part of the ceremony was rehearsed separately until, a week before Coronation Day, set for 2 June, two full rehearsals took place, attended secretly by The Queen, who, comparing them to a family party, said she thoroughly enjoyed herself. Six new musical pieces were

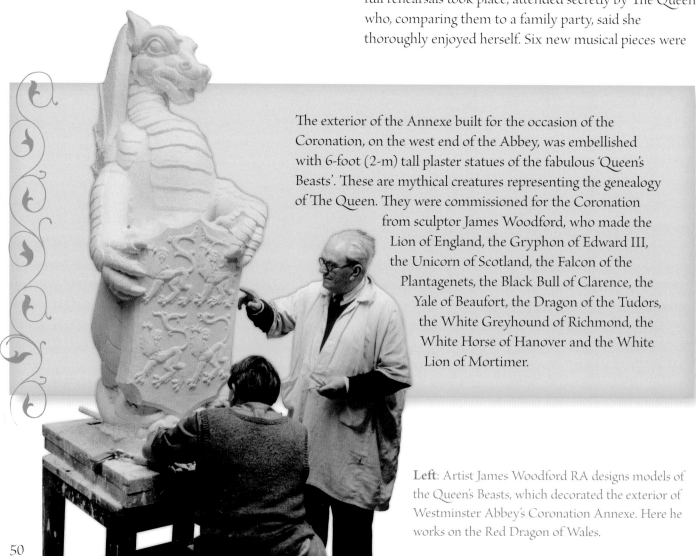

The exterior of the Annexe built for the occasion of the Coronation, on the west end of the Abbey, was embellished with 6-foot (2-m) tall plaster statues of the fabulous 'Queen's Beasts'. These are mythical creatures representing the genealogy of The Queen. They were commissioned for the Coronation from sculptor James Woodford, who made the Lion of England, the Gryphon of Edward III, the Unicorn of Scotland, the Falcon of the Plantagenets, the Black Bull of Clarence, the Yale of Beaufort, the Dragon of the Tudors, the White Greyhound of Richmond, the White Horse of Hanover and the White Lion of Mortimer.

Left: Artist James Woodford RA designs models of the Queen's Beasts, which decorated the exterior of Westminster Abbey's Coronation Annexe. Here he works on the Red Dragon of Wales.

Right: The official Coronation portrait of Her Majesty Queen Elizabeth II and (far right) the dress design by Norman Hartnell.

commissioned under the direction of William McKie, Master of the Choristers at Westminster Abbey. Ralph Vaughan Williams wrote the now classic motet *O Taste and See how Gracious the Lord is*, sung while The Queen took Holy Communion, and he made a new arrangement for the hymn *All People that on Earth do Dwell*. Canadian composer Healey Willan wrote the anthem *O Lord our Governor*, while Sir William Walton contributed an impressive setting for the *Te Deum* and an orchestral piece, *Orb and Sceptre*. Sir Arthur Bliss composed a 'Processional', while Sir Arnold Bax's *Coronation March* was also played. The full choirs of Westminster Abbey, St Paul's Cathedral, the Chapel Royal and St George's Chapel, Windsor took part, along with singers from other choirs. Musical Director William McKie was knighted in the Coronation Honours.

Coronation Day, 2 June 1953

A total of 400 hundred Gold Staff Officers, the Westminster Abbey stewards, were waiting at their posts as the doors opened to guests at 6am on the morning of Queen Elizabeth II's Coronation.

Earlier the eight Yeomen Warders, who, armed with revolvers, had taken it in turns to guard the Coronation regalia through the night, woke in their makeshift beds in the Abbey's Jericho Parlour. The Dean arrived to fill the Ampulla with the anointing oil and it was taken, with the Imperial State Crown, to St Edward's Chapel. The rest of the regalia was carried to the newly built Annexe, to await the arrival of The Queen.

Guests were shown to their seats, conscious that, once there, it would be at least three hours before the service began. As the doors closed to invited guests at 8.30am, the processions from the Annexe commenced, each accompanied by a pair of brightly garbed heralds. First came junior members of the Royal Family, followed by royalty and rulers of foreign states. The rulers of states under Her Majesty's protection came before the Dean and Canons of Westminster, bearing the precious regalia, and bringing more colour with their copes of blue and gold. The heralds accompanied the Princes and Princesses of the Blood Royal, before two more heralds and two ushers led Queen Elizabeth the Queen Mother and Princess Margaret, accompanied by the Lord Chamberlain and the Dowager Duchess of Northumberland, to their seats.

Voices were hushed as the guests sensed The Queen was about to appear. As the chatter died away, the faint peal of the Abbey bells and cheering and shouting in the streets could be heard. Then a fluttering handkerchief was

Above: Her Majesty is greeted as she arrives at Westminster Abbey for her coronation.

Above: The Queen enters the 'theatre' with her Bishops and her Maids of Honour.

the signal to the organist to start playing. Standing by the great West Door, The Queen turned to the six Maids of Honour who were holding her train and said, 'Ready girls?' Parry's arrangement of *I Was Glad* accompanied them as they processed up the blue and gold carpet along the nave. They were preceded by scarlet-robed chaplains, colourful heralds, robed knights and peers, and the Standard Bearers, the Archbishops of Canterbury and York, and the

As Westminster Abbey was opened in the early hours of the morning, Matins, a cat belonging to one of the Canons, was found, fast asleep on the soft cushion of the ancient Coronation Chair.

The Gold State Coach, pulled by eight grey geldings, transported The Queen and the Duke of Edinburgh from Buckingham Palace to Westminster Abbey. The horses were: Cunningham, Tovey, Noah, Tedder, Eisenhower, Snow White, Tipperary and McCreery.

Left: The Gold State Coach, carrying The Queen and the Duke of Edinburgh, processes to Westminster Abbey on the morning of the Coronation.

Duke of Edinburgh. Exuberant 'Vivats' rang out, as The Queen reached the steps up to the Coronation 'theatre' and, at its centre, the Throne.

The Queen stood as the Archbishop of Canterbury turned and faced each side of the Theatre in turn, presenting her to her people, asking for their Recognition. In turn, the congregation shouted approval with the words 'God Save Queen Elizabeth!' Elizabeth acknowledged each shout with a curtsey. Then, seated, she made her solemn Oath to govern with justice and mercy and to maintain the Protestant religion. She was presented with a Holy Bible by the Moderator of the Presbyterian Church of Scotland, who told her: 'Here is wisdom; this is the Royal law; these are the lively oracles of God.'

The most solemn and sacred part of the service, the Anointing, came after the first part of the Holy Communion. Once the Creed had been sung, The Queen, divested of her jewellery and having removed her crimson robe and train and put on a plain white robe, sat in St Edward's Chair while the oil, which had been consecrated earlier that morning, was poured from the Ampulla into the Anointing Spoon. The choir sang *Veni Creator Spiritus (Come Holy Ghost)* and Handel's *Zadok the Priest*. A golden canopy was held overhead, by four Knights of the Garter, to screen The Queen from public gaze, while the Archbishop dipped his thumb in the oil, and anointed her on the hands, breast and head.

After kneeling for the blessing, The Queen was dressed by the Mistress of the Robes, with the help of The Dean, in the traditional Colobium Sindonis and the gold Supertunica and belt. She was presented with the symbolic items of the Coronation regalia, firstly the Spurs and the Jewelled Sword of Offering. She took the Sword and placed

Above: The Queen, wearing a simple white linen dress, sits in King Edward's Chair before the gold canopy, held by four knights, is lowered and the Anointing begins.

Right: The Spurs and Jewelled Sword of Offering are presented to The Queen.

A new batch of oil was made for The Queen's Anointing, after the destruction, by wartime bombing, of the supply last made at the time of Edward VII's coronation. It is made to a traditional recipe said to have been devised for the coronation of Charles II in 1661 and contains olive oil, sesame oil and alcohol perfumed with ambergris, jasmine, civet, musk and cinnamon.

Above: The Archbishop of Canterbury, Geoffrey Fisher presents the Sceptre with Cross to The Queen.

it on the High Altar, returning to her seat, to be invested with the symbols of sovereignty – the Armills, the Royal Robe with the Stole Royal, the Orb, Rings, and the two Sceptres, one with the Cross and one the Dove. Now came the moment of crowning. The Archbishop moved to the Altar to pick up the glittering Crown of St Edward, which had been marked for the occasion with a small gold star at the front to show him which way round it should be placed. The solemnity of the crowning was relieved by a great shout of 'God Save the Queen!', while the peers and peeresses put on their own glittering coronets, the Abbey bells rang out, the trumpets sounded and guns at the Tower of London fired a resounding salute.

Queen Elizabeth II, crowned and steadily holding the Sceptres, ascended the Throne to receive the Homage, first from the Archbishop of Canterbury and then her husband, the Duke of Edinburgh, before the rest of the clergy and peers vowed their loyalty to her. The Holy Communion resumed, before The Queen, carrying the Sceptre and Orb and wearing the Imperial State Crown which she had donned after placing St Edward's Crown on the Altar, processed slowly down the nave. The Coronation ceremony was over.

The first Holy Bible made for the coronation of The Queen's father, King George VI, had been so large that it could not be carried in the procession. The Queen's Bible had a red binding, designed not to clash with the cope of the Bishop who carried it in procession.

The patient crowds lining the streets along the 5-mile (8-km) route back to Buckingham Palace had a little longer to wait before the royal procession wound its way home. Some members of the public had been camping out in their chosen spot for two or three nights. But they were not disappointed, despite the unexpectedly damp and drizzly June day. The procession itself – with Queen Elizabeth the focal point in her magnificent golden carriage – was 2 miles (3 km) long, so that it took at least 45 minutes to pass each spectator. In all, 10,000 servicemen from around the world took part as did 46 bands, some stationed along the route, some marching in the procession.

After lunch in the Abbey Annexe, The Queen donned her velvet robe and the Imperial State Crown, whose four pearls are said once to have adorned Queen Elizabeth I's ears. Her journey home, the coach escorted by a Sovereign's Escort of the Household Cavalry, began along Whitehall, went through Admiralty Arch and then followed a long route via Pall Mall, St James's Street, Piccadilly, Hyde Park Corner, Park Lane, Oxford Street, Regent Street and Haymarket, before returning through Admiralty Arch and down the Mall to Buckingham Palace.

The crowds cheered as the Gold State Coach – accompanied by postilions and footmen, the Yeomen of the Guard, The Queen's Bargemaster and 12 Watermen

The Coronation of Queen Elizabeth II was the cause of great celebration throughout Britain – many people partied in small groups, gathered around newly purchased television sets. Despite opposition, when it was first proposed, that this new broadcast medium should be used to relay the service, the early objections were overcome and the monarchy became part of people's lives as never before. Much of the success of the broadcast was thanks to the adept commentary of Richard Dimbleby, whose meticulously researched explanations of the ceremony and vivid descriptive powers brought the Coronation service, and the sometimes obscure ritual, to life. He admitted he had been nervous about cutting across the words of the Archbishop or The Queen herself, 'knowing that within a second or two something must happen over which one must not speak,' he said after the broadcast was over.

– approached, The Queen smiling and waving slowly from within her carriage. On horseback, apart from the four divisions of Sovereign's Escort, were the Master of the Horse, the Lord High Constable, Gold-Stick-in-Waiting and Silver-Stick-in-Waiting. The Queen appeared to be carrying the heavy golden Orb, the symbolic reminder that the world (the orb) is subject to the rule of God (the Cross); in fact, it was held in a bracket inside the coach so that she could cup her hand around it.

The crowds surged forward to the ornate palace railings as The Queen's carriage turned into the gates of

Left: The Queen, newly crowned, leaves the Westminster Abbey Annexe for the state procession to Buckingham Palace; she carries the Sceptre with the Cross and the Orb and wears the Imperial State Crown.

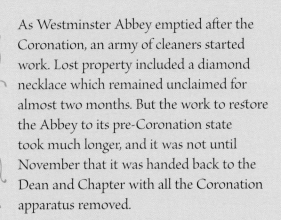

As Westminster Abbey emptied after the Coronation, an army of cleaners started work. Lost property included a diamond necklace which remained unclaimed for almost two months. But the work to restore the Abbey to its pre-Coronation state took much longer, and it was not until November that it was handed back to the Dean and Chapter with all the Coronation apparatus removed.

Above: The magnificent Gold State Coach, dating from 1762, in the Coronation procession.

Buckingham Palace, eager to see her appear on the famous balcony. But they had to be patient, while the formal photographs were taken by Cecil Beaton. As everyone in the coronation party waited for their turn in front of the camera, the pages helped the Queen Mother entertain young Prince Charles and Princess Anne.

The Queen later appeared with the Royal Family and her Maids of Honour on the balcony of the Palace, wearing the Imperial State Crown and the Royal Robes, and

greeted the cheering crowds. Still later, she went out again to signal the switching on of the 'lights of London'. Lights cascaded down the Mall from the Palace, illuminating the huge royal cipher on Admiralty Arch and turning the fountains in Trafalgar Square to great silvery splashes, until all the floodlights, from the National Gallery to the Tower of London, were lighting the decorated streets.

Below: Queen Elizabeth II, members of the Royal Family and her Maids of Honour watch an RAF fly-past from the balcony of Buckingham Palace.

Those who organize and officiate at British coronations know that they do so with the weight of history on their shoulders and the responsibility of interpreting an ancient and hallowed ritual that has been handed down from generation to generation.

These photographs, taken as Her Majesty Queen Elizabeth II was solemnly crowned at Westminster Abbey on 2 June 1953, capture the spirit of the ceremony, showing as they do the Crowning (above left) and the Enthroning.

The Duke of Edinburgh, The Queen's husband, made his own personal homage to his young wife with the words: 'I, Philip, do become your liege man of life and limb.'

The United Kingdom is now the only remaining European country to perform a traditional coronation ceremony as soon as possible after the accession of the new Sovereign to the throne.

The British monarchy is a thoroughly modern institution whose senior members carry out their daily duties with the help of the latest technology. The Royal Family travel to appointments in helicopters and aeroplanes, trains and cars; their progress is mapped by followers using the internet, while their movements are reported around the world by today's super-fast communication. But they still embrace the ceremony and tradition of a great royal occasion enjoyed by all. Out come the golden coaches and carriages, the teams of superb horses, magnificently groomed and apparelled. Out come the pristine uniforms, the sparkling swords and plumed helmets. Scarlet and gold, blue and silver uniforms,

ermine-lined crimson cloaks and gowns make vivid splashes of colour on the greyest of days as the world watches the protagonists in these most British of occasions.

The symbolism of the Coronation, each stage using the glorious regalia and priceless robes kept for this one ceremony, may not always be apparent to the casual observer; however, the solemn and hallowed words that accompany the ritual, the wonderful music, the overwhelming colour and richness of the ceremonial all contribute to the tradition and authority of a magnificent event.

The Commonwealth Tours

Coronation Day was over but the newly crowned Queen Elizabeth II did not rest. A series of visits was planned so that she could meet as many of her subjects, at home and abroad, as possible. The first was in July 1953, to Northern Ireland. The Queen and the Duke of Edinburgh travelled on the Royal Train to Ballymena, Balleymoney and Coleraine, where the train made a stop so that the couple could enjoy the beautiful scenery of the north Antrim coast as they ate their lunch. She and Prince Philip set out in November the same year

Left: The Prime Minister of Ceylon is followed by The Queen and the Duke of Edinburgh at Freedom Hall, Colombo during the royal tour in early 1954. The Queen wears her Coronation gown.

Right: The Queen wearing her Coronation gown in Canberra, Australia, in February 1954. Prince Philip, Duke of Edinburgh, wears his admiral's summer uniform.

to visit Bermuda, Jamaica, Panama, Fiji, Tonga and New Zealand. A further visit in 1954 saw the royal couple travelling to Australia, Ceylon, Aden and Uganda and returning home from Aden aboard the Royal Yacht *Britannia* by way of Malta and Gibraltar. In 1953, the 54 countries of the Commonwealth bought their new Head an exquisite pair of gold bracelets to mark her Coronation.

The year before, in her first Christmas broadcast as reigning monarch, The Queen called the Commonwealth 'a most potent force for good, and one of the true unifying bonds in this torn world'. As she celebrated her Diamond Jubilee in 2012 the Commonwealth Secretary-General, His Excellency Kamalesh Sharma, congratulated her in her role as Head of the Commonwealth, saying that she had been 'the symbol of our free association throughout the 60 years of her reign and is the keystone in our vast Commonwealth arch which spans the globe ....'

The Coronation Ceremony expresses the magnificence of a royal occasion and affirms the identity of a nation and its people. Yet Britain is the only European monarchy to retain this glorious ceremony. When Queen Elizabeth the Queen Mother died in 2002, Queen Elizabeth II remained the only crowned head in Europe. Fascination with the Coronation ceremony and public interest in Westminster Abbey, the magnificent church at the heart of this ancient ceremony, is greater than ever.

At her Coronation 60 years ago on 2 June 1953, The Queen swore to uphold justice and mercy and to defend the traditions of the Church of England of which she is the Supreme Governor. Since that day, she has been as good as her word, serving her people in Great Britain and the Commonwealth with a sense of duty that has not failed from the day she acceded to the throne more than half a century ago.

Unlike the early English Coronation regalia, the Scottish Crown, Sceptre and Sword, collectively known as the Honours of Scotland, were not destroyed by Oliver Cromwell, hard as he tried. They were first used for the coronation of the nine-month-old Mary Queen of Scots in 1543 and later buried for safekeeping, until the restoration of King Charles II in 1660. But they were never again used to crown a sovereign and, after the Union with England, were kept in Edinburgh Castle. The Honours have been removed only once, on 24 June 1953, to celebrate the Coronation of Queen Elizabeth II, when they were taken to a National Service of Thanksgiving at the High Kirk of St Giles, in Edinburgh. During the ceremony, they were carried before The Queen in procession before being formally presented to her. She then returned them to their custodians.

Her Majesty
Queen Elizabeth II's
Coronation Message

On the evening of her Coronation Day, 2 June 1953, a speech made by Her Majesty The Queen was broadcast to the British nation and the countries of the Commonwealth. She acknowledged the ancient origins of the coronation ritual but stressed that the message it gave was as relevant, whatever the year:

'The Ceremonies you have seen today are ancient and some of their origins are veiled in the mysteries of the past, but their spirit and their meaning shine through the Ages, never, perhaps, more brightly than now,' she said. 'I have in sincerity pledged myself to your service as so many of you are pledged to mine. Throughout my life and with all my heart I shall strive to be worthy of your trust.'

Now, 60 years later, Queen Elizabeth II is still serving her people in the spirit of that Coronation message. In return, the monarchy, with The Queen at its head, has been taken to the hearts of the British people, who celebrated in their millions her Diamond Jubilee in 2012, and will do the same to rejoice with her as she marks the 60th anniversary of her Coronation.

Above: Queen Elizabeth in her Coronation robes, the state portrait by
Sir James Herbert Gunn.

Simultaneously published by Pitkin Publishing in the United Kingdom and Dundurn Press in Canada.

Library and Archives Canada Cataloguing in Publication

The coronation : a royal history / compiled by Pitkin Publishing.

ISBN 978-1-4597-1760-2

1. Elizabeth II, Queen of Great Britain, 1926—Coronation. 2. Coronations—Great Britain—History. 3. Great Britain—Kings and rulers—History. I. Pitkin Publishing

DA592.C67 2013 941.085 C2013-900270-7

Care has been taken to trace the ownership of copyright material used in this book. The author and the publisher welcome any information enabling them to rectify any references or credits in subsequent editions.
J. Kirk Howard, President

Printed and bound in Great Britain

Visit us at
Dundurn.com | Definingcanada.ca | @dundurnpress | Facebook.com/dundurnpress

Dundurn
3 Church Street, Suite 500
Toronto, Ontario, Canada
M5E 1M2

Dundurn
2250 Military Road
Tonawanda, NY
U.S.A. 14150

Front cover: The Queen, wearing the Imperial State Crown, smiles as she travels in the Gold State Coach to Buckingham Palace after her Coronation.

Back cover: The Queen and the Duke of Edinburgh greet the crowds, from the balcony at Buckingham Palace on Coronation Day, 2 June 1953.

Inside front cover: The Queen, wearing the purple Robe of State and the Imperial State Crown, holds the Sceptre with the Cross and the Orb, in this photograph taken by Cecil Beaton after her Coronation.